Trinkets Of Reality

The thought of a melancholic mind
expressed poetically, through the rush of life
and the witness of deaths

Abhyudaya

India | USA | UK

Copyright © Abhyudaya
All Rights Reserved.

This book has been self-published with all reasonable efforts taken to make the material error-free by the author. No part of this book shall be used, reproduced in any manner whatsoever without written permission from the author, except in the case of brief quotations embodied in critical articles and reviews.

The Author of this book is solely responsible and liable for its content including but not limited to the views, representations, descriptions, statements, information, opinions, and references ["Content"]. The Content of this book shall not constitute or be construed or deemed to reflect the opinion or expression of the Publisher or Editor. Neither the Publisher nor Editor endorse or approve the Content of this book or guarantee the reliability, accuracy, or completeness of the Content published herein and do not make any representations or warranties of any kind, express or implied, including but not limited to the implied warranties of merchantability, fitness for a particular purpose.

The Publisher and Editor shall not be liable whatsoever...

Made with ❤ on the BookLeaf Publishing Platform
www.bookleafpub.in
www.bookleafpub.com

Dedication

Throughout the end of time, the human mind has been the universe where innumerable thoughts collide every moment as we breathe in and breathe out, with every thump of the heart, the blood coursing through our veins, our imagination leads a path so unfettered by reality, so pure that it needs to drawn through the words we speak, and the ink will feel honoured for it. This is a harmonious tune of words for all those who love literature, who bleed poetry and understand what it feels to write forever and still not feel exhausted in the slightest as the millennia passes.

I dedicate it to all those who wonder if society needs to understand that pessimism is not the dark shadow they fear so deeply but the darkness which makes their light grow brighter. We are the sailors of the ship that fights the darkest battles and still somehow survives the storm to tell a beautiful and pessimistic tale, we don't suffer from negativity, we sit in its warm embrace as it plays with our thoughts make them, the dark saviours we need to forget the scars, we dread.

I dedicate it to those who are the most creative minds of our century but have to fight so many battles on the inside regularly, that they don't even have the energy to pick up the pen and express, I say to those warriors, I see you and I know you, I appreciate you and I know you're trying your best, don't worry you win as long as you continue to have the strength to fight those battles

I dedicate it to those introverts who have the capability to make the world's jaw drop with the artistic capabilities they possess and fear too much, to not do it. At last, I dedicate it to me, the first step towards realising that like everyone else, I am human and I am allowed to fail and am allowed to be flawed, because in those imperfections lies a a mystical perfection.

Preface

Dear readers,

If you're reading this, you already have my gratitude for trusting me enough to invest in me. I if am being completely honest with you, my readers, I believed for a long, long time for almost 15-16 years that I am a deeply flawed person, a fact that was a part of my problems for a while, because I never chose to give myself benefit of the doubt, I realised when I found the world of literature, that we all have flaws and I might be better than I gave myself credit.

This book isn't a group of poems that I just wrote whenever I found the interest or inspiration to, but a memoir, a tribute to myself and my poetic side. The only aim I have with is, that it reaches as many people as it can, so I find other people, people who understand poetry as I do, who don't choose to write poetry but bleed it through the wounds of their past, in such a way that it can be called an art. I agree with Dostoevsky when he said "Pain and suffering are always inevitable for a large intelligence and a deep heart. The really great men must, I think, have great sadness on earth." I grew up reading Geronimo Stilton and I still don't know when that took a great turn how I went from there to Enid, to Catherine Doyle and ended up in the works of Atticus

Aristotle, Nietzsche, Dostoevsky and ended up falling in love with the words and the thoughts these great men portrayed. I don't promise you that my work could ever even come close to those literary legends but one thing I do know. If you read my work, if you really feel the words, reading it again and again, would feel like watching yourself run with those words, every experience with every word, your own and unique to only you, and that's why I believe I need people to read this, so those who suffer the curse of literature, to be able to write pain in words, find respite in this, find peace and serenity in this. In this chaos, that I have orchestrated with the collection of words the best I can. Not every poem might be as long, not every poem as impressionable as the last one. But in case you, my fellow traveller find solace in reading those words, remember, there is another soul just like you, drawn to the darkness, pulled by it but chooses to use it's hues to paint the canvass in such a color that many might find absurd and only a few exquisite, I hope you are one of the few, and I, thank you, for being one of them. This is the start of a journey that is not going to end so easily, I trust that if you join me on this journey, we're going to create a literary haven for the future generations that would be worth witnessing.

Thanking you and always yours

Arthur Mosley (A Poet Of Destiny)

You can contact me for any literary inquiry related to this book, on-

arthur.mosley.poet.of.destiny@gmail.com

Acknowledgements

I have been told by many that acknowledgements are where you give credit to everyone that helped your idea come to fruition. In my life the few people that turned me from a rebellious child, an unmanned force into a person who could use literature to express himself freely. If I had never started telling English stories in that moral education class to impress Mrs. Anisha Pareek ma'am and show her my potential, it never would have built my confidence, if math teachers like Mrs. Richa Varshneya and Mrs. Tamanna Mehta hadn't understood that I was a child that needed their guidance in life a lot more than in mathematics, I still would have been a kid who believed that no one would take a chance on him, thanks to Tamanna ma'am. I was proved wrong and she did take a chance on me. If teachers like Mrs. Vandana Malhotra Surma hadn't taught me to fall in love with English and her lessons from her personal life hadn't taught our whole class to be better humans, we still would have been the wild disrupted kids that were ruined by misuse of online gadgets. Incharges like Mrs. Namita Sehrawat and Mrs. Barnali Roy who saw me be the rebel through years, and used their motherly love to mold me into a better disciplined version of me, I don't know where I would be. If English teachers like Mrs. Jasmine and Dr.

Arti hadn't read every single one of the poems I wrote and told me to channelise it towards a goal and not discard them like I used to, this idea of a book would never have even come to my mind. If Ashok sir hadn't regulated my discipline every single day and taught us Sanskrit so proficiently, I never would have fallen in love with that language. Every single teacher in that institution contributed in changing my life for the better, and it was the best blessing of God to me. They instilled a sense of respect in me of teachers so passionate that I don't think I could disrespect one throughout my life. I had tough times at school but with the teachers there were also friends like Vedant Dandriyal, Hariom Saini, Rajat Rana, Amber Tripathi and Hitish. who made sure I never faced sorrow alone, who turned out to be the most reliable friends I could ever ask for. I have a lot of people I haven't thanked and the list is too long, it feels as if this acknowledgements section has turned into my speech at the Nobel, so I apologise for it's longevity but you would be surprised to know, I didn't even thank so many sweet and important people that came into my life all because of that school and I will always be grateful for it, be it sisters like Meesha Vashisth, Nitya Kumari, Aadya Srivastav, or teachers like Mrs Tripti Maheshwari and Mrs Vandana Wadhawan or juniors. That is it, all the people I acknowledge knowing they're the reason for this book's existence.

1. Curious symphony of scars

I was pulled in by the intoxicating scent of curiosity to
questions my life's reality,
was it as joyful, as I perceived as a child, void of world's
troubles or was that a utopian fantasy?
Wouldn't it be a shame to the giggling child who wished
for a majestic castle for his abode or home ?
To know that the birth of originality through the copious
amounts of integrity, time and honesty, in front of all
made him burdensome,
I walk through the halls of those nostalgia ridden
temples, an atheist, who, every now and then,
shamelessly seeks God's assistance
Wouldn't my 16 year old feel duplicitous, since he used
to have a battle interminable with God, to see me beg for
his nemesis's acceptance?
Would the naive child who always smiled hate me for
taking away his truthful smile and unrelenting joy?
Or would he understand that I wasn't the one, but life's
rough terrains, that, his childhood did destroy

I wonder if peace was nothing but the concept world
made to excuse themselves for their wars? to make sure
they give hope?

Is it too naive, too dream of a time of peace, when ideals
mattered and fervent wishes of harmony danced on the
flames of charity's slope?
It is when I walk through the debris of a vibrant tapestry,
I wonder what my joy used to be, or what were the
echoes of the laughter, that sting now so cruelly?
That maybe just maybe I will try to forgive and forget
the beasts that obliterated me, to try to cover my scars
and try to live anew, become in life a novelty.

Yet, the whispers of the past entwine with each breath I
take, reminding me of light veiled in shadows,
I wonder when will life realise that it empties me, when
it needlessly and thoughtlessly borrows
It makes me curious even so more, does life care of our
conditions as it wrecks our souls and borrows the
fragments that fall to the ground
Or Is it an infallible force which cuts its way through
everything ruthlessly leaving nothing but the story of
joy with torment sprinkled in between as the torture's
bound
Yet the sun still dares to rise, painting gold on the shards,
a reminder that even broken things can glean,
And perhaps, within the ruins of dreams, there's still a
glimmer, a possibility unseen.
even still the human spirit tries to find the music and the
symphony in the chaos that feels eternal and cruel

beyond reason
For that's why one lives, to find the music and dance to
the tunes of the symphony and to the cruel bound
sometimes submit but sometimes commit treason

Woven together the nostalgia of childhood, the
disillusionment of adolescence, and the enduring
curiosity that accompanies adulthood. Questions of joy,
peace, and the scars left by life's battles are not only
personal but universal. In these lines there's an
undertone of hope that persists despite the weight of
reflections—a hope that even amidst the ruins, there's
potential for renewal and growth.
Life is indeed ruthless at times, yet it also offers
moments of unexpected beauty, glimmers in the dark.
Perhaps it's in this duality—the torment and the joy—
that we find the strength to continue, to seek connection,
and to uncover fragments of meaning.

2. Ignorance took my woe

In this world of intellectuals I want to be a simple fool
full of copious amounts of ignorance
that way I wont have to worry about the world and its
problems or worry about intelligence
for all I will care for is food, clothes and shelter and my
joy would be unaffected by the world and its heinous
deeds
and it will no longer be the case that for others misery
and other's stories of woe, my kind and empathetic heart
bleeds
I would be a fool, a laughing at other's humorous fall not
worry about the wounds inflicted,
No longer will I fight for trying to make the criminals
getting away, my story won't be very conflicted

Like an infant I would laugh at every funny face and
flower, but not cry or think about repercussions,
Wanting to do right and voice every crime unnoticed,
being opinionated, would no longer be my passions,
I'll find my peace in ignorance, a bubble where from the
interventions and happenings of the world, my heart can
hide
For dealing with the torturous dealings of the world and
the criminals as a non violent man, I cannot even try to

abide
Am I expected to live in this world without ignoring the
fact that rapists go free but artist don't, is this the rule of
Stalin the dictator?
Isn't being foolish and ignorant to the mere truth of the
treatment of criminals and the heinous crimes they
commit, So easily, an aggravator ?

but how else do I let them be alive if I am not just
ignorant and deny the existence of my woe?
How do I accept the evil this world is turning to, how
magnificently grows my life's only foe...
In a world where not even infants are safe from heinous
crimes like sexual abuse and rape?
I want to be careless and be happy about the country
where the rich can easily, from the law's hands, escape...
you can be mowed down if you're poor and homeless
and all they'll get is to write a paragraph of apology
They try to burn Ravana every year but the forget to
burn the criminals and not an offensive comedian's effigy

As I dance through the meadows, I'll let the rays of
sunlight help me move forward, ask them to be my
guide,
Even If I was a fool who was ignorant, even a fool bears
witness to many storms, that could destroy him and
collide.

In the laughter of little children in their smile, I will find
solace, as I wonder past the truth of life in the beauty of
night,
I'll embrace the warm shadows of the darkness as the
crimes tries to grow itself, let ignorance be my guiding
light.

3. Pick it up, Pick it up, Pick it up

Pick it up, Pick it up, Pick it up she said as she leapt into
the burning fire,
Pick it up, Pick it up, Pick it up she said as she fulfilled
her every desire,
Pick it up, Pick it up, Pick it up he said as his
materialistic identity he did throw,
Pick it up, Pick it up, Pick it up he said as he tried throw
away his woe,
Pick it up, Pick it up, Pick it up they said as they
continued the world's geography
Pick it up Pick it up, Pick it up they said as they gave
away their unrealistic philosophy

Let it go, Let it go, Let it go he said after he ran blindly
after money and greed,
Let it go, Let it go, Let it go he said when he tried to turn
the truth to something ugly, all just to succeed
Let it go, Let it go, Let it go she said as she fell into the
societal hatred and beauty standards of the society
Let it go, Let it go, Let it go she said as she tried to accept
as a gift, in truth given by people as an unwanted reality
Let it go, Let it go, Let it go they said as they tried to
hold on to your secrets, scars and tears

Let it go, Let it go, Let it go they said as they tried to add,
everyday, something new to your list of fears

Put it out, Put it out, Put it out they said as the burned
high the fire of judgemental hatred and discrimination
Put it out, Put it out, Put it out they said as the pushed
down every aspirer and killed art's culmination
Put it out, Put it out, Put it out he said as he tried to fight
the rising waves of pain of self hatred
Put it out, Put it out, Put it out he said as he tried to use
creativity and break the stereotypes sacred
Put it out, Put it out, Put it out she said as she desired to
lead the way to feministic freedom
Put it out, Put it out, Put it out she said for not wanting
to be a house wife and their home her only kingdom

Run away, Run away, Run away, she said as she tried to
give up all her dreams due to societal pressure and the
want of some how being enough to someone's
expectation,
Run away, Run away, Run away, she said as she started
to be numb to the pain that her own family left her in
inheritance and her being weak, feeling unwanted
depraved of their validation,
Run away, Run away, Run away He said as the society
pressured him to marry someone at the right age, while
he figured out his career and being extremely successful

all at once,

Run away, Run away, Run away He said as every one expected him to man up and never express emotion, to feed his family his sole devotion and while being subjected to emotional, physical mental and societal violence

Run away, Run away, Run away They said as they completed their torture and ended the story of one more child all because he couldn't get a suitable rank in their examination

Run away, Run away, Run away They said as they completely destroyed both the genders, suppressing them equally with different expectations from each leading to nothing but the person's destruction to their satisfaction........

4. I search for you

O heavenly peace that stole my heart,
the silent song that pulled me apart,
I search for you, I search for you,
the siren song that left me spell bounded

As I measured the edges of the moon lit lake,
that showed so much peace,
I search for you, I search for you,
the angel whose beauty left me astounded

those beautiful eyes of the infant
that saw deep in my soul, and smiled at me,
I search for you, I search for you,
those eyes whose judgment I loved so easily

that playful dog that jumped at my sight,
that let me pet and caress him without a single fight,
I search for you, I search for you,
that peaceful creature who loved me so innocently

to those field of roses, thorny but beautiful,
that are worth bleeding such a magnificent spectacle,
I search for you, I search for you,
those fields that draw me like a call to depart

In those trees that hold, centuries of memories
every man that sat under, a thousand stories untold
I search for you, I search for you
the stories that resuscitate my heart

5. Nastenka's woe

That man from the town of Saint Petersburg who told me
his dreams and listened to my ode,
Who understood my life and sorrows in his dreams and
eyes made my wonderful lovely abode,
The story of my life pinned to my grandmother's side,
waiting for my bleeding heart, to return to my caress,
In desperation of his return, I would lament to that man,
as he told me his unique dreams and his heart's address,
But his affection unrequited and so was mine for long, to
return to my heart's on his arrival, did, feel, ever so
wrong
And the man from Saint Petersburg, like mist, did drift
away but It felt so hurtful as my soul to that man
couldn't belong

Even though I had the right to see that quirky dreamer
as the brother to adore so well,
But we shared what the connection was in our souls so
common, to be cast in loneliness's shell
I wish to be as if that deaf servant who accepted my
command to beside my grandmother, by whose side I
spun life's wheel,
O how the dreamer adored me so precious and how he
must have stifled his flame that burned his self, As my

love's return I did reveal
Yet in this silence, where desire and desperation dance,
our fates intertwined like vines, I mourned the words
unsaid between the lines of our souls, caught in the web
of unbroken signs
I wonder how I found such a masterful dreamer and how
he understood me every turn and more, How I found
such a symphony when life had already written my
personal musical score

As I leave for the final encounter with that dreamer with
hopes and love for you beyond explanation,
All I will wonder is If the root of all relationships that
ever exist in love actually a need, a desperation
For what is love?, other than the unending desperation
to be understood and have a witness for one's life
But the destruction of the heart of the dreamer and the
pursuit of my heart, was my eternity's inevitable strife
As I left that broken dreamer on the rooftop of our starry
nights where the words sang and stories fluttered,
I went with remorse in my eyes and his hearts fragments
left on the floor, there was a smile for my happiness on
the broken dreamer battered

6. The Pot of Life

So do you ever wonder, that if we're all just earthen pots
dropped from the sky
when we're born each broken in a different ways but
some people's fragments are completed by other
 and they together continue to complete each other and
hold the water of life,
Like my mind goes to the thought that sometimes the
fire of passion solidifies those pots further
and helps them hold the water longer while some people
try to force the fragments together as their original soul
chips away
only to crack after a while due to the pressure of the
circumstances and stress of commitment,

while some intentionally do so to submit to a person
completely as they believe it the way they can atone
to the point that they would rather mend the cracks than
be broken alone.
But what if the pot was broken to begin with like what if
all of life is just the plot full of despair,
where every now then there is a pot that turns out to be
more broken beyond repair,
and the fragments are so small that the pieces as much as

you try slip your hands like the smallest pieces of sand,
for I really wonder is life fair? Is it a maiden trying to
bless everyone with the an amount of woe and joy they
can withstand?,
or is it a warden watching over all of us trying to make
sure we don't cheat someone out of it? or all we are is a
bunch of dreamer until the hopes eventually burnout
All those broken pots ever wonder if they will ever be
able to hold the stable water of life or
will it be the tide that wipes them out.

Like what I don't understand is why we would rather
wear the mask of duplicity instead of being authentic
and original with someone ,
is all relationship nothing but a façade two parties play
until ones real colours weep into the floor and witnessed
by the other, the life's backbone?,
and what then, it's not as if we as humans are
invulnerable to pain and emotional attachment and
aberrations,
in fact it is one of the pillars that holds up the human
life. So in truth all pots are too broken to be fixed except
a few exceptions
and all we could wish for is the sweet release of death
after having a witness throughout our whole life,
be it our parents at first then our life partner, our

children to witness us trying to be alive.
To witness us being alive and not suffering....

16

7. New Beginnings

I wonder how it all started, and how it still continues,
doesn't life on Earth have so many hues?
Do we all have some chances to grab at the opportunity
in front of us and just miss the subtle cues?
Life is not just a sorrow to ponder over in a state so
dejected, but also a wonder filled with joys,
Wouldn't it foolish to not witness the beauty but only
what life in wrath so ruthlessly destroys,
Its a force of destruction and growth for one cannot exist
without the other's presence
If a plant grows, someday a tree that formed the fruits
that gave its seed will die, is Life's fundamental essence,

When an infant is born, its indicates its arrival in tears,
and releases a wave of joy in the parents hearts,
Similar to pain of loss, but isn't it similar to the subtle joy
for the suffering's end when an old soul departs
In this dance of existence, we realise that every now and
then life lights flames of dissonance with our situation
Every brushstroke on this canvass of life is precise
whether we think it a irregularity and a cause of
frustration
Yet even in that chaos, there lies the spark of creation, a
symphony unfolding, rich with collision,

From ashes to blossoms, as the seasons sway, each
moment a verse in this grand composition,

A song of time is too sweet and too painful to always
remember, to each, is sung a unique one,
In melodies woven through laughter and sorrow's soft
tether where every heartbeat echoes a rhythm that
cannot be undone.
So dance to the notes of your story, embrace every high
and low, let each heartbeat guide your motion,
For in this intricate tapestry of life, we find our purpose,
a constant wave upon the ocean.
So raise your gaze to the expansive skies, painted
brilliantly bright with the colors of hope and renewal of
our reality,
Embrace the unknown with open arms, allowing your
spirit to take flight into the realms of infinite possibility.
For every new beginning presents itself as a precious
promise, a remarkable chance to embark on our unique
journey,
To dance with the future, to dream boldly, and to
advance with unwavering faith in the beauty of what lies
ahead.

8. The dying embers

I stood in front of that burning pyre dying for the wish
to be the human burning inside, so raw, so pure is fire,
burns everything away and nothing to hide
What was that fascination with that inferno that lied in
those flames, with every degradable particle turning to
vapour, as if the corpse was cleansed with fire
A lifetime reduced to ashes, as the son gave fire to his
father, every relative that didn't remember that corpse
for years decided to gather
I sat after a while witnessing the man I knew my whole
life was gone in a moment's interval, the person who
was supposed be in my marriage died before 12th's result
As the people started to leave the cremation ground, as
the fire still burned so bright, as the bones that were left
to turn to dust, I wondered why humans are selfish to a
fault
We pretend to be righteous to be always trying to be a
better person, but deep inside we're all selfish to want
personal gain, even though there are a few exceptions
the crackling sound of the fire that burned, that ember's
glow burned in me a want to selfless, for the smokes
drew up the memories of my grandpa and my
mischievous sessions
the Maggi he would wait for me to cook, so we could eat

together in our house when my parents were out for
something important, the stories he would tell me of the
man he was, so respected
the chowmein and momos that whenever I would order,
he would instantly know I did, and even though he
wouldn't say he liked it, the idea of me giving him a part
of it, from him was never rejected

the man, who would take pride in telling others about
how, the grandson, gave him, the big expensive burger,
he would eat in peace in the park in secrecy
as his laughter would mingle with the rustling of leaves,
the joy to know that he was his grandson's partner in
crime, a confidante, wasn't a bond one could forget easily
every time I would order food non vegetarian , the pure
brahmin in him, would never get angry but smile and
laugh to see me enjoying, to him, what was, a forbidden
delicacy
each bite, a bridge between our worlds, uniting legacy
with laughter, as flavours intertwined, the warmth of his
wisdom tucked in my heart,
what love we used to share, was seen when he went to
the hospital ICU, dropping tears as he saw me in that
condition, a forced smile whenever I'd depart
I was the one he held dearest, as the smoke that grew
that went up and curled away from the pyre,
each flicker of the flame, as I sat through that process,

every single memory got caught in the mire
I grasp at the empty void where his presence used to be,
where his laughter used to dwell,
and I find myself constantly still rejecting and
questioning this unending farewell
I will carry him forth with me as he was my dearest too,
and in me, would always be, his essence entwined,
in the stories I tell everyday that I breathe, in the tales I
make to cheer up the lost, in every moment of kindness I
find,
for hopefully for me his legacy will continue to live in
me and every ode that I write, in each choice that I
make,
and the laughter we shared of the mischievous deeds
innumerable, is memory that I hope, it will never break.

so here's to the moments as I leave the dying embers of
the man he used to be, both fleeting and bold,
to the essence of love that we had and shared and even
the fights in between are stories, that can never be sold,
to the memories of him and his life as my grandfather,
no matter how faulted at least he tried wrapped in joy
and in pain,
the cycle of life continues as it will, no force to ever put a
pause to it, but only the memories where love shall
remain.

9. The Brightest Night

why was this night not so peaceful what was so serene
in the darkness yet so hopeless
why was my heart drawn to this, this night so
unconventional, a night without darkness
The stars couldn't be seen anymore the light enveloped
their presence in that sky so beautiful completely
That moon that was every love's hope and who inspired
poets lost its wounded shine and burned too abjectly
Those thinkers that slept on their roofs at night to sing
for life's peace, were scared away by the bright sky and
lack of stars
Those poets who wrote of the moon while listening to
the stars were gone now like an addict trying to quit as
he threw away the cigars

Not many understood this darkness that was gone, for
not many could appreciate its beauty so wonderful and
its song so serene
it was a unique pain to understand that darkness, to
listen to the whispers of the silent stars, to wait
for them to talk and understand what they mean
It wasn't a justification of pessimism, trying to create an
attraction to the cues of the dark and to inspire in ones
heart the delicious taste of negativity

But a respite for those who wandered with masks telling
the world of their joys and selling them on dreams when
only they understood their reality
It was something as simple as a battered soul to tired to
live from the pain it experienced in the joy that is known
as life and its want to rest for a while
It was something so complex that when those going
through it heard about it, they wouldn't describe their
pain or talk about it, just give their best smile

The night gave birth to the bright day that was a truth
undeniable but those who considered only positivity the
truth, considered the dark an excuse
But what could those hearts know, which danced in light
and sung its songs about those wounded
hearts that the dark gave a peaceful refuge
Why wasn't moon's darkest side that's never seen talked
about as romantically as the shining side
because in darkness is the true emotions abode
It's easy to love the brightest parts of person's soul but to
learn the darkest wounds of one's soul and see the scars
is where lies love's truest ode
One can easily love the best parts of a person but its
difficult to understand and love the flaws that we put so
much effort to hide and keep away
When one is able to handle the the darkest day and the

brightest night is where one often may act like they
don't, but need all their strength to array

24

10. The God Almighty

When the ritual of society dragged me to one of the
many of homes of my religion's god, I went reluctantly
to pray for some respite and joy
but when I entered the steps of the temple, I felt it an
effort futile for this was the same almighty who was
praised for his miracles not blamed for what he
destroyed
As I lit the incense that would please the goddess that
was set in front of me in stone, I wondered did milk,
water, incense and other all the penance that one needed
to do to atone?
When I circled the temple, repeating the god almighty's
name, is when I wondered to back of mind, did god
instruct these people to not let the harijans enter the
temple, to give them nothing but shame alone?
Did those people who fight for the sake of reservation,
ever think what the minorities went through, what
discrimination they faced, how they are still treated
lesser than, still considered not ideal for marriage?
Because I was one of those fighters, and I sure didn't
until I saw the rural society, and I saw the people who
were so educated, feel disgusted by the thought of
marrying a "lower caste", I hated this unnecessary
disparage

wasn't he the one who caused millions of catastrophes or
is it all forgiven for he is our master and whatever he
does is the best to be, whatever happens to the rest
if god's all just, evil will cease to exist, if god's all
merciful no criminal could ever resist, if god is all
powerful, he couldn't be the best, if god is all good, then
the devil is more powerful
for power exists outside the bounds of morality, if morals
existed beside power, one couldn't have the capability to
do something that morals don't allow, hence with power
one cant be the best
if god's justice is just for everyone, then criminals
wouldn't exist, but god isn't all merciful too, for then no
criminal would ever be punished, hence god is a complex
too mystical
for those who suffer with the curse of knowledge, many
couldn't believe in god, for he is the respite that controls
this society, without his hope this world could easily fall
apart,
but man only acts as if there is no free will, to control his
darkest urges he grabs onto the control of religion, for
his reality morphed by the existence of a mystical figure,
a punisher
and isn't man, nature's deadliest monster that we all
know within some deep corner of our mind and heart,

but the day man realises himself as the apex predator, all
morality will depart
even now some men act on their darkest desires, those
monster are banished publicly to instil the fear in other
monsters' hearts, to make them realise what other
humans are capable of, and what punishment the world
will deliver

It was when I saw my mother telling me to give alms to
disabled man, that sat on the outskirts, I wondered what
the world's view of the disabled at least in our country
had come to, this day
Even though people like Srikanth Bolla, Sudha
Chandran, Girish Sharma, and millions more proved us
wrong about the people specially abled and still there are
many children who think begging is the only way
Then I wondered if god exists then why doesn't he
bolster the confidence of those with shattered hopes and
dreams that died due to the different events of life, but
then who cares it's just a beautiful day

11. Devil's Innocence

My mind's curious imagination about the presence of divine justice led to me a slumber yet so wonderful, that it showed me the dream where the devil proved his innocence in the court of man

the story initiated when a man who considered him the humankind's advocate and challenged the devil, that he will prove him to be the root of all evil, when furious but intrigued fallen angel agreed is when the duel began

all of mankind witnessed as once who was the god's favourite son, and the fallen angel, came down to the mortal plane and wore the guise of a human as he stood in the defence of his honour

The man began his statement by calling upon him, as the root of all evil, the mischievous voice that sat on every human's shoulder, the cause of all sin and due to whom humans lived in pure horror

the devil smiled as the man continued to defame him calling him everything that is wrong and the one that caused all the misery and suffering in the life of humans, the originator of all lies and blasphemy

the judge listened to the long urges in the statements of the advocate as he continued to condemn the devil and insisting that he was the reason that every evil ever existed, even the darker forms of alchemy

The devil sat in pure silence as the man tried to paint the
canvass of his profile in the court feeling more than
amused in the attempts the man made to convince
everyone
He knew that man understood that once his statements
were done, would come a being that according to him
lured everyone into sin and could influence anyone

After the man, finally sat down, done with his efforts
hoping to make a step towards the long perilous journey
of success, rose the devil to make his case
He asked the world to answer him if they agreed with
the advocate who presented his case just so passionate,
many shouted in agreement, while others were silenced
by fear's embrace
He then inquired why the world who blames him so
passionately never saw the aspect where he was god's
favourite son, or the aspect where he was the first one to
protest for free will,
Wasn't he just the excuse they gave the pesky little voice
in their head, that told them to be good, a reason to
escape from being good and blame the sin on him while
they enjoyed the thrill
Is there no difference in their minds between the
punisher of evil and the representative of evil, for all of
mankind, the warden of hell, was blamed for every crime
that man. in his senses, committed

How hypocritical were these people who call him the
root of all evil and reason for all their sins, but never
chose to think to not obey his "influence" onto them if
they were good, and all sins were hated
Wasn't it their choice every time a heinous human
decided to brutally assault another human's offspring, if
not why was he punished? or was the devil wasn't the
excuse to commit sins as told
The warden of hell, the realm made for those who
committed sins so gruesome was, yet again being blamed
for the deepest darkest urges that controlled humans
since times old

So I command you to throw your stones and light your
torches to make your decree but question yourself, for
once without the devil, who would you actually be?
For in this duel that you so desire intensely, and the
banishment of your sins to me, you so hungrily crave,
you forget I am but a mirror reflecting the depths of your
misery
what of the envy that festers like a parasite in every
mind where innocence bloomed, what of your greed that
flows like a river so wide consuming this planet so blind
Is it I who sows the seeds, or do they burst forth from
your own soil? Is it my smile that tempts or merely the
hunger for what you cannot hold? is my question to
your kind

Unclench your fists, dear judge, and look within, For
what shines brightest may also harbour sin, does not the
light cast its own shadow or even that my evil trick?
I am here, to tell you the raw truth as it dances in front
of your eyes, I don't care for victory but hope that every
right word causes pain in the criminal mind with every
prick
Thus, the court stood still, suspended in thought, after
the feeling of shame filled the hearts of the humans, who
tried to blame the devil, while the devil's laughter
echoed, tasting sweet victory,
In a battle not of righteousness, but of the truths we
hide, and as the ink began to dry on fate's eternal scroll,
the line blurred, and the soul of man embraced its role
understanding morality was not a mystery

12. The Animal Child, My Mirror So Wild

As I walked down the stairs of one of the many homes of
my religion's deity
I laid my eyes at that child jumping around, such a
masterpiece, a thing of pure beauty
It wasn't so brave to disturb the worshippers that
wandered around him, nor too afraid to wander at the
precipice
As I went near him, he sensed my presence and ran so
swiftly as he was followed, by me his excited accomplice
He wasn't a slow beast, as the fear kicked in, as he ran, I
ran by his side until he stopped at the edge of the
institution,
I knew that to earn his trust wasn't an easy task and I
didn't care as still I felt as unknown and unreasonable
devotion,

I plucked leaves to bring to him, for I knew he must have
wanted to eat, with that run, he must have been
exhausted,
He was a bit sceptical, ready to flee again at the moments
notice, for his trust in me was still something to be
attested,
As he nibbled on those green luscious leaves, I was lost

in those blue oceanic eyes and caressed his wounded
soul,
When he came close to me in trust, to eat those leaves, I
felt we united together, two mammals as one whole
He rested his neck on my knee, as I fed him leaves and
patted his fur while scratching his head, to help him
unwind,
In this creature I met, what felt like moments ago, I
would have without any second thought betrayed all of
humankind,

I sat on the steps of lake beside the home of the deity
only the child and lake in my mind as I introspected in
peace and serenity
I fed those leaves to that beautiful child, who embraced
me in return, the most uncomplicated and magnificently
serene
part of my reality
As I got up to leave so remorsefully even though I loved
everything related to this, every part of nature around
that child so naive, left the leaves to follow me, for it
never knew our relationship was never outside time's
bound
When I started to leave, that child jumped in sorrow
looking all around, screaming for me in pain, as if I was
his father,
Why did it pierce my heart, to see that child looking for

me, knowing it was even without, the most painful departure,
Before I left I wondered if the theory that all relationships are based on a selfish need and desire, a theory too ridiculous,
For that child so starved, left those leaves for me, searching so woefully, his hope to be with me, a hope too ambitious...

And in those fleeting moments, I felt the weight of existence, a bond forged from innocence, pure and untainted,
He felt so helpless after finding some love and affection, in the end separation from it, is what his fate's canvas painted
In that sacred space, beneath the gaze of the ever-watchful deity, two beings shared a truth less known to all mankind,
That love, in its truest form, is not bound by reason or need, but exists in the heart's gentle pull, tender and kind.

13. The story of a misunderstood spider

As I walked through the forest I saw a ferocious spider,
the critters would cry about his terror, the bugs trembled
in his fear, they called him a monster yet too powerful
but when I ignored all those warnings, and went ahead
to meet the creature without no prejudice, instead of a
monster that the forest feared, I found him weaving
webs extremely delicate and beautiful
I sat and witnessed the art he created yet so effortlessly
and the way he considered his abode in the webs yet so
graceful, it felt the world told me everything but the
spider's peaceful reality
But why was this creature then so feared and and
repulsed when I felt nothing but peace and serenity in its
presence, why was the artistic spider forced to live a lie,
a travesty?
I wouldn't speak a word for a long while as I watched the
spider grow his threads that shimmered in the sun like
morning dew, light and grace danced on each strand
The spider had noticed me too, but was too engrossed in
the art's culmination to greet the foreign entity, but after
while in a raspy voice the reason for my presence he did
demand
I smiled and wondered whether to be honest and then

decided to be, I told that the animals sung tales oof his terror, how monstrous he was, But with my own eyes, I wanted to see,
But All I saw was an artist who effortlessly made the most beautiful art with his web, a predator yet to so peaceful with eyes that sparkled in the sun's graceful light, like an eternal beauty

He thanked me for my honesty and then went silent for a while, while looking at the green forest where he was feared, and then said "I was taught fear lasts longer than love... A lesson I never forgot"
"I am not a monster they call me to be, but in this nature, one has to be ruthless for their survival, they call me out for striking fear in others, as if they never in self preservation, had a selfish thought,
Its easy to pass judgement as if one is the most honourable but the hardest to critique one's own tale, If even a single one of them saw a moment of weakness in me, they would do their best to end me without fail
I am a survivor who wanted to be loved and treasured for the art of web, but just for my terrifying appearance and my huge figure, even the most fearless animals who came to visit me, in a prejudiced fear would turn pale then why, O wonderful human, do you not fear me or run at my sight, what ability do you have, to see past my

hideous appearance and see my peaceful nature, and love
my artistic side
How do you find beauty in my eyes that scare everyone
out of my home, those webs that seem to everyone as a
beautiful trap, and me, as soon as they see, they run to
hide.."
For I am a human, considered the nature's greatest
monster, we destroy everything that nature gave the
world, and don't even try to bother, to leave anything
better as if the planet our inheritance
you're not a monstrosity to me as all you try to do is
survive, while us humans continue our exploitation even
though we thrive, and when we see the adverse
reactions, we try to cling to a defence
The art you create with what nature gave you is the best
thing possible in your fate, as you're channelling what
this mother nature gave you and trying to be a peaceful
creature yet so serene
No matter what other animals think of you out of fear,
for what life teaches every mammal, one day to be
curious and not prejudiced said the traveller as he
listened to the spider's tales and everything in between...

14. The sorrowful horse

There was a stable that housed the finest horses, but one of those horses was known, not for its agility or for being a pure bred, but, for, being a horse full of woe See, the horse wasn't born on the farm with that stable but was one with the wild, found by the utter fabulous way in which he ran, defeating any and every foe Although, the issue was the horse didn't have foes, only friends, the group of horses that he ran with, were the only friends he ever made and lost due to their lack of agility

The horse which used to make fun of his friends, racing them while he left them in the dust, so proud, was now sorrowful at all times, losing them, all due to his cursed capability

The fields he once wandered, so joyfully as they were the shadow of his pride, were now haunted by the laughter of his lost friends which echoed like screams from which he couldn't hide

Whispers of freedom, that now, were made in the silence of the night, were once the thoughts he considered a fundamentality, something now tethered and tied

When his masters would leave him out to pasture, knowing he would come back, he wouldn't rest like he needed to but search for the companions that made his world bright

every forage and every green forest which used to be the
grounds of the games they played, beneath the wide
open skies that were the sore eyes' favourable sight

Now in the bright sun, he toils alone, O how must
mother nature fret at his misery,
Her winds whisper gently, weaving through
branches, each rustle a reminder of the camaraderie
Yet everyday he hopes as the master puts on the blinkers
for him for his job to begin, to be lost and never found
that one misted morning he would, perhaps, find that
dirt path to those he lost, those to whom freedom never
knew bounds
And so he gallops, with his heart so heavy, yet the spirit
still stirring, beneath the vast sky, yearning for the
sound,
Of hooves that once danced beside him so joyfully, their
laughter and freedom as if it was a symphony
profound.
In dreams of twilight, he chases the shadows of those
friends, their faces etched through his mind in the fading
light,
A promise is made to the evening stars by him everyday
that one day, he'd join them, to once more take flight.

Have you seen that woeful horse, for it lives in every

heart, the hearts that killed their passion and left their
friends behind to be the race horse of their sort
but deep inside every one of them know as it runs with
its blinkers on, chasing every target, like a machine yet
too familiar no matter how much the effort
I wish in with every woeful horse that lives in someone's
heart, there comes a person with the freedom chasing
horse in their heart to throw the woe away
For when the master will put you to pasture that friend
might be the one you're looking for everywhere but by
your side, and I hope they make you stray

15. Love, wish it could be

How is it that the child who was denied the gentle
spoonfuls of love,
found solace in the cold embrace of knives whose edges
whispered pain,
learning to savor the cruel banquet of blood and anguish
he dreamed of,
for even in the smallest morsels, he discovered solace
within the disdain.
Why does love, that mercurial and elusive creation of
human fragility,
become the poison we so desperately crave, though it
corrodes us whole,
its dual nature weaving joy and sorrow into the tapestry
of our reality,
while loved ones' derision leaves behind shadows
imprinted on the soul.

What sacred essence does love possess, that its absence
carves despair,
transforming life's vibrancy into gray desolation, an
abyss none escape,
as if its radiant presence alone could redeem those
beyond repair,
its light casting vivid forms amidst a void of hollow

shape.

Perhaps it is not the presence of love, but the agony it leaves behind,

a gaping hollow where its melody once sang, now echoes only grief,

for even in its cruel departure, its haunting absence begins to bind,

making wounds immortal, each scar telling a story beyond belief.

The child, who once kissed the blade, knows not to mourn its wounds,

but instead he grieves the absence of tender hands that could cradle,

for what is love but both warmth and torment, comforting then consumed,

a fire that burns bright and beautiful, yet disfigures those unable.

And yet, in the absence of love, he carved his sorrow into lines so stark,

turning pain into poetry and anguish into fleeting art that stayed,

for only those who bleed with pen in hand can find light in the dark,

transforming chaos into words, their torment never betrayed.

Love, so often sought as salvation, reveals itself as both

gift and curse,
its paradox inescapable, both healer and destroyer
entwined,
its venom laced in beauty, leaving its mark in every
verse,
a reflection of its duality—unforgiving, but divinely
designed.
To those who wander loveless, adrift in silence colder
than the night,
know that the ink you spill is a testament to battles
fought alone,
every word a fragment of survival, forged in the absence
of light,
each poem a monument to a soul that rebuilt its broken
throne.
For through the trials of love, and even in its cruelest
form's decay,
art arises, a sanctuary for those who bleed and
persevere,
and though the scars it leaves may never truly fade
away,
they shine as emblems of strength, a beauty only pain
can engineer.
And so, the child who tasted knives now paints his
wounds in hues,
transforming anguish into colors only kindred souls
perceive,

for in the chaos of suffering, a rare masterpiece he imbues,
and though the world may falter, his art will never grieve.

16. Superheroes of my life

I know of a child that used to dream of the stars when he was 7,that child that promised to be everything that is right with the world and a superhero in a league of its own, life's sweetest fantasy
But that child turned out to be faulted and damaged, as the seedling grew from the promising bud to a dying sapling, a joke in contrast to what he dreamt of, so shortly ago, of what he used to be
Every thing that was wrong with the love starved child was that the family that was supposed to protect him from the world so cruel, ended up being just as similar to the world so inhuman
The child who ran everywhere trying to pour his soul out for a bit of love, got nothing but the truth of the supposed real world which worked on being selfish to a child, an act too barbarian
But the wounds were healed, for with existence of hatred, there was also love for that child, but only the love of the educators who were nothing but angelic to the child rebellious
Every time the child lashed out expecting them to leave, they punished him for it, they taught him to be better, they stayed, they listened and they never judged that child so cautious

When everything went wrong and the situation was
difficult at his domestic life, when all he had was pain to
see, he never expected that he would, actually, with
assistance, whether the storm
In time he fell in love with the teachers that turned him
into all the good parts of him, in them he saw the
motherly love, he craved so intensely, the one he begged
for, but was never worthy
He found a human connection in a few teachers that
made him feel that institution was his true home,
be it the disciplinarian, who stopped him at every
misstep, made him socially healthy
or the lovely literature teachers who nurtured his soul
and made sure he reached his potential
or every moment the teachers of science let him be,
knowing he was forced into the realm of physics and
chemistry
or the way the maths teachers understood him, and his
grasp to reach for the stars and showed him support
beneficial
for if the teachers never helped that little seedling to
grow, or help him stumble through the forced years of
science
those teachers taught him the art of living, to be
respectful and happy and in life some good people or
angels do exist

the institution that employed them, wouldn't have been
his home, the best part of a very troubled and tense
adolescence
they took a damaged a soul that was hurt, and helped
him heal a significant part of him, even though he did
resist

To be that child and hear words of appreciation from the
teachers, he considered as divine angels, was a
symphony to his ears so sweet, it burned a little hatred,
he faced
Every mistake he made, he never felt sorry to anyone but
only to his teachers, whose expectations, he wanted to
exceed, to be worthy of their love, and their pride was
the only achievement he chased
The moments he won a medal, or a trophy, his parents
reaction wasn't a concern,
but his teacher's smile, their joy at his victory was a
badge he felt honoured beyond reason to earn
All, I wanted to be, as that child so conflicted was to
fight my way through life and wage wars on every
imposter that supposedly cared for me, so they would
leave eventually
But those teachers were the best part of my life, taught
me to be what I am, a peace was ignited by them, as they
with love changed everything that surrounded my
reality

Those teachers were lifelines, anchors in a stormy sea, helping that child not only survive but also grow into someone capable of appreciating life and human connection. Their presence speaks to the profound impact that educators can have, proving that love and guidance don't just come from families; sometimes they bloom unexpectedly from others who care in ways you never thought possible.

17. NTA and its endless maze

In the tender bloom of youth, they rise to chase their dreams that gleam with unyielding zeal and light,
 But the path before them bends and twists, a maze of uncertainties that stirs their souls with fright.
Books tower like monuments in their rooms, each page holding the key to futures yet unseen,
 While pens become their mighty swords, battling endless questions on this relentless routine.
NEET and JEE loom like formidable gates, holding the promise of futures both bright and demanding,
 Yet modifications strike like untamed storms, shaking their foundations and leaving them unstanding.
The rules evolve faster than the world turns, creating waves of confusion in every fragile plan,
 And syllabi balloon beyond comprehension, leaving clarity shattered like dreams upon the sand.

Late into the night, by the dim glow of flickering lamps, they study with the stars as their loyal guide,
 While the world beyond their windows slumbers peacefully, unaware of their struggles they cannot hide.
Silent cries escape their lips as walls absorb the pain of hearts burdened by countless trials untold,

Yet they fight alone in this arena of solitude, forging
dreams in silence as their fire takes hold.
Parental hopes linger like the breeze, whispering of
perseverance and futures that must unfold,
 Their sacrifices weighed against societal demands,
forcing them into molds both harsh and cold.
"Be the pride of the family," they hear, as expectations
bloom into gardens too vast to contain,
 Yet despite the storms, they march forward, carving
paths through the darkness beneath skies of rain.
Friendships offer fleeting solace, comrades in arms who
are also rivals chasing their singular prize,
 Together they laugh in rare moments of peace, yet apart
they battle the doubts that silently arise.
Mock tests become a battlefield of ranks and scores,
where every mark etches lines upon their fate,
 And the weight of competition presses hard, breeding
doubt and sorrow as victory comes late.

Yet within their hearts glows a fire unyielding, growing
stronger with every scar they wear with pride,
 The maze twists and turns with unending challenges,
yet their resilience refuses to let despair decide.
They find fleeting triumph in moments of clarity, where
answers unfold like light breaking the dawn,
 And in these victories, no matter how small, their
courage is reshaped and their fears are withdrawn.

Dreams flicker like fragile flames amid darkened nights,
as doubts and fears press sharp and cold,
 Yet every failure blooms into lessons profound, pushing
them forward with determination bold.
The tempest of fate tries to fray their resolve, yet hope
rises like a phoenix breaking through stone,
 And though the weight of the world's gaze remains,
they press on, undaunted and remarkably alone.
When the gates swing wide and dreams are unbound,
they'll emerge as warriors carved from struggle's flame,
 Triumphant in battle and proud of their scars, carrying
the weight of victory etched in their name.
For the system may test their breaking point, but it
cannot quench the fire burning deep inside,
 Their resilience paints the future bright, a legacy of
courage and dreams their efforts amplify.
Through NEET's trials and JEE's endless maze, they
stand as examples of willpower profoundly strong,
 No storm, syllabus, or twist of fate can dim the
brilliance of their determination lasting long.
Their journey becomes a tale of strength and hope, a
testament to the spirit of youth and dreams untold,
 And the maze, once a barrier to their ambition, becomes
the foundation where passion takes its hold.

18. The Jade Masterpiece

The silk like tendrils of the lotus flower, giving rise to the
masterpiece where world is made of mud and soil,
luscious green leaves that surround the trees, adorning,
which grew tearing the soil and lived the birth of
turmoil,
The sharp thorns of the beautiful magnificent rose,
protecting the infant while it blooms its absolute beauty
It pierces the hands of the one who tries to pluck the
rose, like a loyal determined soldier never abandoning its
duty,

I wonder if mother nature made us in the image of a
monster, since all we do to her is exploit and harm
beyond repair
Or I am just a bleeding heart, adorning my mother, who
is perplexed to see and disturbed know about much we
add to her despair,
In the tapestry of existence, where love and pain entwine
are the hidden stories of these beautiful lives of our
siblings yet so different,
The forest frog, the deepest eyes sitting on a wet leaf,
where even the smallest stone goes under, is a balance
yet so unique and reverent

as the deer watches the water from a eye filled from
thirst, is a mind that wonders the fears that the predators
might lurk to end its journey and hence lies in patience
Ferocious tiger hiding in the camouflage stalking the
prey yet so delicious and valuable for his survival, is a
predator that lives on the sole instinct and experience
Was this all not the poetic nature's poem and all this a
beautiful painted art? are we so engrossed in exploiting
this home that we grew so far apart?
As the beautiful swan, has the ability to drink milk
mixed in water so easily, aren't we all the opposite
running for the water, when the nectar of gods is the
milky part?

Can we not see the fragile thread, the bonds between us
and the mother, yearning for tenderness, calling for a
future bathed in light?
Aren't we intertwined souls, one with our mother, need
to feel the anguish that we cause our mother, worsening
and deepening her plight?
We need to want to witness the stars in the night, that
one day could be without pollution that we caused if
only I could be back in that hometown untouched from
the city's modernity,
Awake, my brothers and sisters, for we need to break
this slumber of indifference and continuously harming,

our lovely patient mother who waits for us in pain to
want to change this reality

54

19. सामर्थ्य

क्या देवो का यह खेल है क्यों हम ऐसे असमर्थ है ?
क्या यही जन्म की देन है क्या स्वेच्छा निरर्थ है?
जो धर्म को थे पुजते बने राक्षसों से बेहूदे ,
क्यों नारियों कहीं सुरक्षित नहीं , क्यों पूज्य घाटों से भी वो डरे?
क्या धर्म को बचाएंगे जो खुद को न सुधारते ,
काम क्रोध लोभ ईर्ष्या से ये सज्जन रोज़ हारते

पवन की शीतल हवाओं में प्रदुषण के भर गए निशाँ,
क्यों रासायनिक पदार्थों के आदि हो गये आजके किसान?
जो नदियाँ कभी जो देती थी खेतों को पानी जन्मती बहार,
आज हमारे कर्मो के कारण झेलती प्रदूषकों का अत्याचार,
नारियां जिन्हे पूजते थे जैसे देवियां निज्जीवन का प्रकाश
बन गयी वो महिला जो खो रही स्वतंत्रता एवं सुरक्षा की आस

परन्तु क्या को देवों को फर्क नहीं जो निर्मित हुआ नर्क यहीं
वो नन्हा बालक कैसे इस दूषित दुनियां में समझेगा क्या गलत क्या सही
क्या हम कह सकेंगे उस छात्र को की हमारे देश में हर नारी है देवी सी?
जहाँ रोज़ छपती घटनाएं बलात्कार की , कही अपहरण और शोषण तो कहीं हिंसक जीवन साथी?
क्यों अपराध हुआ इतना लिंगहीन की मनुष्यों ने मचाया हाहाकार
क्यों नर भी जीवन खोते प्रतिदिन, क्यों नारियां भी बानी गुनेहगार?

आखिर देवों का ये खेल नहीं सब हमारा ही सामर्थ्य है
एक दूसरे की सहायता कर्म सर्व अहम है दोष बाटना मूर्खकर्म
एकाएक सबसे व्यर्थ है
परयावरण और स्वजीवन को भी. सुधरने की क्षमता हम में ही
परन्तु मुर्ख कम नहीं है जो जीवन इसी में व्यर्थ करेंगे की कोन गलत
और कोन सही
आखिर क्यों न बनाएं हम, ऐसे सवेरा जिससे बहे स्नेह? जहाँ नारी का
अस्तित्व हो, न डर की हो कोई पेहचान,
गूंजे जीवन में खुशियों की, बहे प्रेम और सम्मान। क्या हम कुछ ऐसा
कर पाएंगे, जहां हर दिल हो दीवाना?
जो मुठ्ठी में बंधा हुआ है, वो आकाश में उड़ान भरने दे,पश्चात्ताप और
चुप्पी को, एक नई आवाज़ में बदलने दे।
इस चिंतन में निहित है शक्ति, है उन्नति का रास्ता नया,क्या हम अब
खुद को बदलेंगे, या हमें रहना है पुराना?

20. सत्य

क्या सत्य है मूल इस जीवन का आज एक कथा सुनाता हूँ
क्या शौर्य है सत्य के संलग्न में एक काव्य में तुम्हे दिखलाता हूँ
एक चोर था अतीव कौशली खुद के गुणगान गाता था
चोरों में वो धूर्त चोरों का सम्राट कहलाता था। वो था इतना प्रभावशाली
की दुर्जन उसकी प्रशंसा करते थे
फिर वैभव अपना दर्शाने वो साधु के भेष में राजा के राजमहल गया
राजा ने भी उसको देखा तो उस चोर को न पहचान सका साधु समझ
उस ढोंगी को उसने पूर्ण सम्मान दिया
वो गंभीरता से बोला हे राजन मै बुरी खबर एक लाया हूँ जो नहीं सुना
मेरा विचार तो यह देश नहीं रह पायेगा
जो प्रजा तुम्हारे संतान सामान उन पर गहरा बादल छायेगा
राजा भी थोड़ा घबराया भय में बोला हे साधु क्या करना है आदेश
करो कोनसी विपत्ति ऐसी है जो मेरी प्रजा को सताएगी
कोन सी ऐसी आंधी है जो मेरा मुकुट गिराएगी
वो साधु मंद मंद मुस्का कर बिला हे राजन मै राह में हमारे देश की
और बढ़ती शत्रु सेना देख के आया हूँ जो निश्चित शीग्र ही आएगी
 हम सब प्रजा के सज्जनो पर एक गहरा घाव लगाएगी जिस आपत्ति
से तुम हो भयभीत वो आपत्ति को लाएगी
अगर देश तुम्हे बचाना हो मुकुट को अपने त्याग दो मै राजा नहीं एक
साधु मुझको ये राज्य दान दो तुम जूठ कपट का साधन लो और
शत्रुओं को मात दो

राजा भी ज़ोर से चिलाया और बोला की ऐसा उचित नहीं मै सत्य की
राह न त्यागूंगा सत्य ही मेरा गर्व है सत्य ही मेरा धर्म है

और उसकी रक्षा में मै लड़ जाऊंगा

मेरे सत्य में मेरी शक्ति है ये मैंने बाल्यावस्था में सीखा था चाहे मृत्यु आजाये दर पर मै फिर भी युद्ध में जाऊंगा उन दुह्शासि शत्रुओं को सत्य की राह दिखाऊंगा

ऐ साधु तुम ये जानलो मेरा सत्य है मुझ में अमरगीत उसको कोई नहीं चुप कर पायेगा ऐसा कोई दुष्कर्म नहीं जो सत्य को कभी छुपायेगा जिसका दीप जलता है हृदय में, वो अंधकार को मिटाता है, करता है जो विजय, स्वयं पर जो यकीन रखता है उसको ईश्वर भी साथ निभाएगा

हर तूफान को सहकर, वो अपने के लिए खड़ा होता है मैं सत्य की धरती पर, धरूँगा विजय का परचम आज, साधु तेरे भेष में छिपा सत्य, मैं उसे पहचानूँगा।

न ऐसा कोई महंत हो जो सत्य की राह से भटकायेगा तुम ने क्या ही ज्ञान अर्जित किया जो ऐ साधु मुझे कायरता सिखाएगा आखिर तुम कैसे कह सकते हो की असत्य की राह मुझे सफलता दिलाएगी असत्य का वास नरक में, केवल धोखे की बुनाई है मै तुम्हे जीवन में परिवर्तन करने की सलाह देता हूँ, हे ढोंगी यह तो तुम भी समझगये की सत्य है जो जीवन का, वही सच्चे सुख का जश्न मनाएगी।

वो चोर भी समझ गया और हार उसने मानली जो चोर था कौशल पर करता गर्व अपने उसने राह बदलने की ठानली

अब सरलता में वो एक नई दृष्टि पाकर,सत्य के संग अपने जीवन को सजाने लगा,जहाँ असंख्य पथ खोले थे, अब वो उन्हें पहचानने लगा। सत्य के मार्ग पर चलकर, गर्व वो था अज्ञानी, अब सजगता से स्वीकार कर, वो बना एक सुन्दर कहानी।

21. हार मानूंगा नहीं

तुम मुझको यूँ नकार दो चाहे मुझे तुम कितनी हार दो मै हार मानूंगा,
नहीं हथियार छोड़ूंगा नहीं ,
इस जीवन की रणभूमि में कई मुश्किलें जरूर आएँगी कुछ अधिक
घाव देंगी, कुछ रास्ते दिखाएंगी, चाहे जो भी मेरी कठिनाई हो, मै हार
मानूंगा नहीं हथियार छोड़ूंगा नहीं
इस राह में जो ज़िन्दगी कई फ़ासले यूँ आएंगे जो मुझको मेरी उम्मीद
और आशाओं से हर रोज़ ही बिछरायेंगे चाहे कितनी भी हो दूरियां
उनका साथ छोड़ूंगा नहीं, मै हार मानूंगा नहीं
ऐ शत्रुओं तुम जानलो जब मुझसे लड़ने आओगे चाहे कितना भी तुम
ठानलो तुम्हारे बाण कितने भी हो क्यों नहीं मेरी चाह को चीरेन्गे नहीं,
मेरी जीत छीनेंगे नहीं
कई मोड़ ऐसे आएंगे जिनमे बेबसी मुझ पर छाएगी कई दिन भी ऐसे
आएँगे की पराजित होगा मन का भाव लेकिन ऐसे दिन के बाद भी मै
चलना छोड़ूंगा नहीं, मै हार मानूंगा नहीं
मन के भाव से वास्तविक हार है उसको नियंत्रित जो तुमने न किआ
तो मन की एक हार पर झट भुज चलेगा हर दिया मै ऐसे मन से
जीतकर ए जलाऊंगा फिर यही, मै हार मानूंगा नहीं

ओ मेरे युवको, फिर उठ चलो ! हर हार से तुम फिर लड़ो! क्योंकि हार
हरदम आएगी तुम्हे नइ राह इक दिखाएगी जो राह तुमे ने देखली और
जीत तुम ने चाहली, तो हार मानना नहीं, हथियार छोड़ना नहीं
हार का भी एक स्वाद है जो अपरिहार्य है अनिवार्य है ये स्वाद जिसने
न चखा उसने प्रयत्न ही किये नहीं हार के बिना कभी विजय संभव
नहीं पर हार से न हारना, तुम इस स्वाद से न भागना

ज़िंगदी के पथ में तुमको कठिनायां बोहत सी आएंगी कुछ मृत्यु का भय दिखलाएंगी तुम भय का कंठ दबाकर अपने भय को दिल से त्यागना और भ्रम से भय के जागना

हर अन्धकार और प्रकाश में चाहे खुश हो दिल या निराश है तुम आस को न छोड़ना उम्मीद को मत तोडना जो कार्य तुम लगे रहे तो सफलता तुमको चाहेगी और मुश्किलों की राह में राहत की वृष्टि आएगी

बस एक ही आग्रह है मेरा हार मत तुम मानना चाहे कैसे भी परिस्थिति आजाओ तुम खुद को सक्षम जानना तुम वीर वो पराक्रमी जो हर युद्ध में विजय पायेगा, तुम ग्यानी हो भुद्दिमत जो सर्वोच्च ज्ञान पायेगा

www.ingramcontent.com/pod-product-compliance
Lightning Source LLC
Chambersburg PA
CBHW070553160726
48003CB00005B/2028